Erik

BOOK CLUB EDITION

The Big Jump
and Other Stories

Written by BENJAMIN ELKIN

Illustrated by KATHERINE EVANS

Beginner Books
A DIVISION OF RANDOM HOUSE

G   H   I   J   K
0 1 2

THE BIG JUMP

In the old days, no one but a
King could have a dog for a pet.
So the King had all the dogs in
town. He had big ones and little
ones, thin ones and fat ones.

When the King took his dogs
out to play, the boys and girls
would all come to look.

Then one day a pup ran away
from the King.

It ran to a little boy. The name of the boy was Ben. Ben bent down to give the pup a pat on the head. "Go back!" he said. "I am not a King! Go back to the King!" But the pup gave Ben's hand a lick. It would not go back to the King.

"Look at that!" said the King.
"My dog likes you. It is too bad
you are not a King. If you were
a King, you could have this dog."

"How I wish I could have it!" said Ben. "Could *I* be a King? What do I have to do to be one?"

The King laughed.

"Oh, a King has to do a lot of things," he said. "For one thing, he has to know how to do the Big Jump."

"The Big Jump?" asked Ben.

But the King was gone!

Then Ben saw him way up
high on top of his palace!

"How did you get up there?"
asked Ben.

"All Kings can jump like this,"
said the King. "If *you* could jump
up here you could not be a King.
But you *could* have the dog!"

Then the King came back. He
looked down at Ben.

"Would you like to have that
dog?" he asked.

"Yes, I would," said Ben.

"Well, you may take him home
with you for one day," said the
King. "See how high you can
jump. Then come back. If you
can jump to the top of my palace,
you may keep the dog for a pet."

"I will do what I can," said
Ben. "I will go home and see
how high I can jump."

11

When Ben got home he took some jumps.

He could jump to the top of one box.

He could jump to the top of two boxes.

But he could not jump to the top of three boxes. He and the boxes fell down.

Then Ben took a big stick to help him jump.

It was a good trick, too. Now he could jump high. He could jump to the top of three boxes. Then four boxes.

But that was as high as he could jump.

And then the pup did a funny thing.

The pup jumped up on one box. From that box he jumped to another, and then to another. When he got to the top box, he looked back at Ben.

Ben laughed. "Good, good pup!" he said. "Now at last I know how to do it! Come, we will show the King that I can jump to the top of his palace."

Then Ben went back to see the King.

The King was on top of his palace.

"I can do it!" said Ben to the King. "Like this!"

Ben jumped up the steps one by one. Jump, jump, jump. Step by step to the top of the palace.

The boys and girls looked at Ben. They laughed. "We can *all* do it *that* way!" they said.

19

"Yes," said the King. "*Now* you can all do it. Ben showed you how. I did not say that Ben had to do it in *one* jump—and he did not. But he did jump to the top. So the dog is his."

"Oh, thank you!" said Ben.

"And thank *you,* too," Ben said to the pup. He bent down to shake the paw of his pup. "You showed me how to jump up here.

"I will name you JUMP. And you will be my pet from now on!"

And that is how Ben came to have a dog in the days when no one but a King could have one.

SOMETHING NEW

In the woods, Ben and Jump could hear a funny thump. Thump! THUMP!

It came from a big, deep hole. Ben and Jump looked. Someone was down there! It was the KING!

The King in a hole?

The King did not see them.
He came out of the hole.

They could hear the King say,
"The thing that I want is not in
that hole." Then they saw him
run up the hill!

When the King got to the top of the hill, he looked around. He looked high. He looked low.

"Oh dear," said the King. "Oh, no. The thing that I want is not here on this hill."

"What is it you want, good King?" asked Ben.

But the King did not hear him.

Then Ben saw the King run
down the hill. He saw him take
off his gown. Then his crown! He
put them down. Then he went
into the lake!

The King looked around in the water. "It is not here," said the King. "The thing that I want is not here. Now, I do not know where to look."

"But what IS it you are after, good King?" asked Ben.

"I am after Something New," said the King.

"How new?" asked Ben.

"Oh," said the King, "this has to be *so* new that *no one* has ever seen it before!"

"Why do you want this new thing?" asked Ben.

"It is not for me!" said the King. "It is for the bad King. He will be at my palace at noon. If I do not find something new by then, he will take our gold."

"Do not give up," said Ben. "I
will do what I can."

"Thank you," said the King,
"but I fear it will do no good."

And he got out of the water
and went back to the palace.

At noon, the bad King came
to the palace with all his men.

"Show me something new,"
said the bad King. "If you can
not show me something new,
give me your gold!"

The good King was sad. "I
fear I have no new thing to give
you. Take my gold, if you will!"

BUT THEN....

Ben ran in with a box.

"The bad King will get no gold from us," said Ben. "I can show him something that *no one* has ever looked at!"

"How can that be?" said the bad King. "How can you put something in a box and not see it?"

"I do not know what is in the box," the good King said. "But this boy knows how to do things. Ben, give him the box."

The bad King looked in the box. All that was in it was one little egg. But then, as he looked, that egg gave a bump and a shake! And out of the egg came a new little chick!

"Look there!" said the good
King. "That chick is as new as
can be. No one could ever have
seen it before! Now, be gone!
You can not have our gold!"

Away went the bad King with
all his men. After him went the
little chick. There was not a
thing the bad King could do.

He had something new. So he
had to go away with no gold.

And the good King laughed.
He said, "Ben, I will name this
SOMETHING NEW DAY.
From now on, all of the town
will look for new things on this
day. With your help, we will
find them."

THE WISH SACK

One day Ben met a funny old man with an old black sack.

"Good day," said the man. "We men of the woods want to give you this Wish Sack. You can wish things into it. Wish for something. Then say, ABBA, DABBA! And what you wish for will be in the Sack."

"Thank you," said Ben. "Well, I do wish I had a new hat.

"ABBA, DABBA!"

Ben put his hand in the Wish
Sack. And there was the hat!

"Thank you," Ben said. "Oh,
what fun I can have with this
Sack!"

But back in the woods was the
bad King. And he saw all this!

"Say," said the bad King, "I
could have fun with that Wish
Sack, too. Then I could wish
things into it. I will have my
men get it for me!"

The next day three of the bad King's men came to Ben's house.

One man took hold of Jump so he could not bite.

Another man said to Ben, "Can you help me? Look at my little pig. He is sick."

And then as Ben looked at the pig, the other man went into the house to get the Wish Sack.

He ran out of the house with
the Wish Sack in his hand.

Jump saw him and got away
from the man who had him.

Then Ben saw the man, too.
The man ran as fast as he could.

"Stop! Stop!" said Ben.

But the man ran on.

And Ben ran after him.

49

"Hold on there, Ben!" It was
the good King who said this.

"Do not run after those men,"
said the good King. "It will do
you no good. The black walls are
high! And the bad King has lots
of men. But I can help you get
your Wish Sack back."

And then the King told Ben
what to do.

And when all in the black palace had gone to bed, Ben said, "Now?"

"Yes!" said the good King. "NOW!"

"ABBA DABBA!" said Ben.

"I WISH THAT I WERE IN THE WISH SACK!"

Pop!

And Ben was in the Wish Sack.

He was in the Wish Sack in the bad King's black palace.

But WHERE in the palace?

Ben put his head out to take a look.

He was in the Wish Sack on the bad King's bed!

The King was asleep. But would he wake up?

Ben had to get out of that Sack.

He had to take that Sack and get out of the bad King's palace! FAST!

Ben got out of the Sack.

Step by step, like a mouse, he went.

A man went by.

Would the bad King wake up?

A cat went "Meeow."

Would the bad King hear it?

Ben had to get out of there fast!

The King did wake up!

He saw Ben with the Sack in his hand.

"Stop that boy! Stop that boy!"

Ben saw three men come at him.

Ben threw the sack out and let it fall. Down it went!

"ABBA DABBA! I WISH TO BE BACK IN THE WISH SACK," said Ben.

POP!

Ben was out of the black palace, back in the Sack again.

"You did it," the good King said. "Now get up here with me! We will go to my palace."

And they did.

After that, the good King let
Ben keep the Sack at his palace.
And Ben let all the boys and girls
come and make wishes.

"ABBA DABBA!" they would
say. Then *POP!*

All the things they wished for
were there in the Sack!